"I Am Enough"

Is B.S.

THE TRUTHS YOU NEED TO BECOME MORE...

Liz Lima

This book is dedicated in memory of Tia Maria Fatima Machado Resendes. You were an incredible woman. You always had the desire and fire to get things done. You mean a lot to me. You will be forever missed.

Copyright © 2019 LIZ LIMA

All rights reserved. No part of this book may be reproduced, stored in a retrieval system, or transmitted in any form or by any means, electronic, mechanical, photocopying, recording, scanning, or otherwise, without the prior written permission of the publisher.

Disclaimer

All the material contained in this book is provided for educational and informational purposes only. No responsibility can be taken for any results or outcomes resulting from the use of this material.

While every attempt has been made to provide information that is both accurate and effective, the author does not assume any responsibility for the accuracy or use/misuse of this information.

Some names have been changed and/or omitted in order to protect the privacy of certain characters in this book.

Table of Contents

INTRODUCTION..13

Chapter ONE: THE EPIPHANY: HATING "I AM ENOUGH" 21

CHAPTER TWO: CARPE DIEM: RIGHT WHERE YOU ARE 49

CHAPTER THREE: THE PAST IS JUST THAT........65

CHAPTER FOUR: PHOENIX HOUR......................89

CHAPTER FIVE: END THE BULLSHIT: WHAT'S YOUR PLAN?...113

CONCLUSION: THE VENUS WARRIOR 143

INTRODUCTION

Dear Venus Warrior,

I will never tell you that you are good enough.

Does that sound strange to you? Well, that's a good thing. Ok, you may be wondering how and why being told that you are not good enough is a good thing. The truth is that you are MORE than enough, and the sooner you begin to live with that reality, the easier it will be for you to reach inside you and identify your unique strengths. Or as you will discover in this book: your inner Venus Warrior.

Before you proceed with reading this book, I need you to look into the mirror and tell yourself this: "I am better than enough. I have so much inside me, and I am ready to discover my Venus Warrior." You need to say these words with enough conviction until you believe them, and they become ingrained in your psyche so much that they become a part of you.

You need to do away with the words "Enough," and start thinking of "More."

It is important to note that society is more comfortable with having you tell yourself that you are enough, and that you have everything you need. While there is really nothing wrong with that statement, a problem arises when you have doubts deep down within you and you know that you may not be all that, after all.

How many of you, like me, walk into a store and see a poster or something with the phrase, "I am enough" on it? How often do we go on Facebook and see things like that? We hear people that we know state loudly, "I am enough!" And yet the more we know them, more importantly, the more we know ourselves, the more that we know that we don't feel like enough. If anything, we've used the phrase as an excuse to become more complacent, living our lives on a wish and hoping things will miraculously get better just because that's what we desire. As a matter of fact, this mindset is responsible for a good number of people becoming so laid back that they do nothing at all. After all, if you are already enough, then there is no need to do more or try to do anything at all, is there?

The "I am enough." mentality is a very attractive excuse to just get by, not putting in any effort to be a better person, to improve on your qualifications, gather more skills and experience or even improve on your relationships. It is really just living in your comfort zone and being unwilling to do more. I have lived with this mentality, and so I know that just getting by is not enough; rather it is a gross underutilization of your gifts and will leave you yearning for more deep down within you.

Hey! It is true that we all want to feel good; so even when we are not doing so well, the natural impulse is to push the blame on external factors. We would rather not have to face our own inadequacies head-on, and this is why we tend to become complacent with the resulting effect that we don't try to be anything more at all. The problem is not with society, the problem is with us and what we have chosen to believe and accept as our reality: the lazy confession, "I am enough".

As we go through the pages of this book, we are starting a journey that will help you discover just how you can beat the odds, overcome your default state of being complacent and move on to becoming a better you. I will be sharing my story and how the lessons I learnt from my experiences made me determined to find a solution to my unease and how I was able to discover my strength from within - my Venus Warrior.

There's so much more inside of you which empowers you to achieve all that you want to achieve in life. Life's challenges will come your way and you will have the highs and lows that accompany making life choices, but the most important thing is how you react to these things. As a woman, you are expected to be several things at the same time. To be a successful woman, a super mom, the perfect wife, partner, and so much more. Without doubt, this is a lot of pressure for anyone to go through. However, you can go through it all and come out stronger than ever before. This is where the Venus Warrior inside of you will find expression.

You have been too laid back over the years, letting life happen to you instead of happening to life and living on your terms. You may have unconsciously allowed the external noise to drown the voice of your Venus Warrior, making her quiet and subdued; rather than the strong, vocal and unique voice she was meant to be.

Now is your time to take up the call to be empowered, to achieve all that you are meant to achieve. It is high time you embraced your Venus Warrior and begin your journey to fulfilling your heart desires and making an impact in the world. It is time to let go of the pretentious statements, the façade that you wear so no one knows what is truly going on inside you and embrace your authenticity. This is the only way to walk away from life's bullshit feeling empowered and turning it around for your good.

Are you ready to go on this journey? I hope you are because I have so much to share with you and I am confident that you will find the answers you have been seeking and the lessons shared in this book will point you in the right direction.

Let's go, Venus Warrior!

Chapter ONE: THE EPIPHANY:

HATING "I AM ENOUGH"

In our journey through life, there will be several defining moments that will alter the course of our lives; this could be in a good way, or in a bad way. Each of these moments is made up of events, or a series of events, that may be related or isolated. However, the way you react will determine the eventual outcome. I have had a few of those defining moments, but the one that stands out the most and which is the most relevant to the current discussion was what happened to me one of those days when I made a trip to Staples to get some supplies.

Over the years, I formed an attachment to motivational quotes. They have actually been helpful to me in my life's journey. So, I became a sort of collector, always on the lookout for keepsakes or souvenirs with powerful quotes and one-liners on them. Actually, I have tons of folders, binders, and pens that have motivational quotes written on them. Some of the most popular ones include "Make today amazing," "I'm so awesome today that yesterday is jealous," and so on. I had several items that had variations of these quotes and similar ones, and I was not done collecting them.

However, on this fateful day, when I entered the store, it seemed like all the items on display had the words "I am enough" printed on them. The words were on everything and everywhere I looked inside the store. After a few minutes in the store, something snapped inside of me and I just could not take it anymore. It felt like I was hurting deeply on the inside, some old mind wounds were being reopened. And in a flash, I was transported back to those times in my childhood where I was bullied and scared. I was taken on a journey through all my insecurities in a split second, and that made me extremely upset and angry. At first, I was angry at the world and how untrue the words "I am Enough" were, but after a few moments of introspection, I had an epiphany.

The reason was quite simple; "If I am enough, then why am I even trying?" I mean, there should not be any need to worry about anything, or aspire to be better at anything, or to be anything at all, right? That means I have everything I need, and I can just go through life without making any extra effort. If I was enough, why then did I feel so inadequate? Why was I having such strong and weakening reactions to memories I thought I had long buried and dealt with? Why did I constantly aspire to be more?

This was the moment everything changed, and I began to see my life through a whole new lens. I am not enough, because I am constantly growing and that is what matters. The desire to be more than what you currently are, is very important and will be the driver for most of your life-changing decisions.

This was my epiphany. I hated just being enough, I had to break away from the norm that wanted me to remain in my comfort zone; I had to take some bold decisions so that I could be in charge of my life. This was the moment my Venus Warrior was revived, and I started this journey.

My life changed in that very instant and the series of events that followed were simply physical manifestations of the changes that already took place inside me. Your life can change in an instant; however, you have to be prepared to seize the moment and make the best of it.

It is important to know that there are no hard and fast rules about getting an epiphany about your life. You don't have to wait for your own Staples experience, or wait for something out of the ordinary to happen in your life. You can have an epiphany at anytime and anywhere; you just have to always keep an open mind and be prepared to make changes in your life.

Imagine just how sad it would be if we had a life where we do not really know who we are, where we never know the feeling of really loving ourselves or being able to achieve our dreams; imagine if we were in a life where we do not realize that it is not okay to just be "enough." Rather we have to keep pushing and aspiring to greater things. What a waste that would be.

Here's one truth you need to know: Spending so much energy on being "enough," is an absolute waste. Rather than being inspirational or motivational, the statement and mindset is actually limiting and can stop you from evolving and developing your full potential. Even if you do not currently feel it, you must believe within you that you are incredible, and being just "enough," will not cut it for you. You were destined to be more. And until you arrive at that point and allow your mind to go through a paradigm shift, you will be stuck at the same point without making any progress.

Why is it important to have an epiphany?

An epiphany is a mental moment of immediate clarity which can result in you taking action to change something about your life or to change the course of your life's journey. An epiphany isn't always a pleasant realization; sometimes, our eyes are open to things we would have probably preferred to not know or things we feel we are probably better off without. Yet, at the end of the day, what matters the most is how we use the epiphany we get.

It is important to note that all epiphanies are not the same. Some demand a deep reflection that requires you to ask yourself tough questions, and your epiphany will depend on what your answers to those questions are. In some other intakes, the epiphany is so fleeting that you may miss it if you are not attentive.

In my experience with the women I have worked with, so many of them are searching for a big "Aha" moment which they will be able to tie the change in their lives to. Here's the thing, not everyone will have an "Aha" moment, and not everyone will have a "Staples moment." No, it does not make you any different from the other people around you. One thing that is clear, though, is that everyone has that mind changing moment, no matter how subtle it is.

When you get an epiphany, the next step is what you choose to do with your newfound clarity, and how courageous you are to actually act on it.

In the course of my life, I have discovered that epiphanies are important for several reasons, and these reasons, when taken singly or collectively, form the major reasons why most people want to have an epiphany.

Firstly, an epiphany helps you to recognize that you are the most important court when it comes to deciding cases about yourself. What I mean is that your opinion of yourself is what matters the most, and not what other people think about you. How the world would perceive you is ultimately your choice and you are the only one who can project the image you want other people to have of you. People will only see you as what you have chosen to identify as, so you have to show them the real you. Of course, this is an epiphany in itself and one that everybody needs to have. When you have arrived at this point, you are definitely one step closer to unveiling your Venus Warrior.

Secondly, you will be better positioned to understand why sometimes you do not really need to struggle so hard to make things work out for you. You will recognize that option A is not always the best or only choice, sometimes, option C may just be the winning hand. The universe always works in favor of those who understand its rules and bend them to their own will. Your choices do not always have to cost you something for them to be valid; if something appears too draining, then maybe it is time to let it go. You do not need to be uncomfortable or super stressed just to prove that you are making the right decision. Yes, people will say the road to success is full of ups and downs; but who says you have to keep holding on to something that is no longer working for you or helping you grow? When you realize this and have evolved to the point where you can let things go when they have served their purpose of when they no longer serve a purpose, then your Venus Warrior is getting super charged and is ready to take her place.

Also, you should come to a realization that being alone does not mean that you are or should be lonely. In the course of your journey, there will be times when you have to go it alone; this does not mean you should start panicking and looking for ways to surround yourself with people. There are parts of your journey that simply do not involve other people. It is also an avenue to learn how to enjoy your own company and overcome the fear of being alone. Your Venus Warrior is an Amazon who knows how to fight alone and with people when needed.

When you get an epiphany, you will understand that your journey is more important than the goal; in other words, how you get there is more important than getting there. It is quite simple: this is how you grow, change, transform and become a better person- you become 'more'. There is no doubt that smashing your goals is important, but your journey is equally important. So, ensure you keep your mind open to soak in the process for all it is worth.

A good number of the women I have worked with were only able to discover their purpose during the course of their journey to revealing their inner Venus Warrior. Yes, they had passions that they wanted to work towards; but, until they became open and attentive, they did not discover their true purpose. Each step on your journey is deliberate and regardless of how painful the process may be, you should savor it and make the best of that period.

How does having an epiphany change your life?

Oh well! It doesn't. That's another truth you may not hear too often.

An epiphany will not change your life! It is not a magic wand that just makes things turn around the way you want them to. So many people are chasing after epiphanies with the hope that it would lead to some magical breakthrough in their lives, help them end a crisis or provide some deep insight into their lives.

I hate to burst your bubble, but the epiphany you have will not do anything for you. Well, it will not do anything for you until you take the right action and steps. The truth is, you are the only one who can change your life. YOU HAVE THE POWER, and that is what discovering your Venus Warrior is about.

The way an epiphany works is that it causes a paradigm shift, which could be a slow process during which the real breakthrough happens. So, you get an epiphany about a particular thing, like I did in Staples, that "I am enough is bullshit," but what do you do with that realization? For me, I started Venus Warriors with a vision of inspiring other women and helping them reach their own goals. I did not wait for some external force to make things happen, I was proactive and acted on the realization I got.

It is important that you do not get intimidated simply because you feel other people have gotten clarity on the course of their lives while you are still trying to make some sense of yours. Enjoy <u>your</u> process and make the best of it.

Life is undoubtedly going to be full of challenging and tricky problems, and you may not get the clarity you need at the exact moment when you are chasing after it or craving it. However, it will come.

So, do not wait for an epiphany to change your life. It won't.

The only way your life will change is when you take charge and start calling the shots. This involves you accepting that you cannot change external circumstances or people, but you can change yourself. It requires a great deal of inner strength to come to this realization and to work with it, and this is what your Venus Warrior will help you achieve.

Building Your Inner Strength

How often do you wish you had greater willpower or inner strength? How many times have you made plans to change your life, but things didn't quite work out like you expected? Do you wish you had more strength to follow through on your dreams and action plans? Are there strong and resilient individuals that you look up to because they have shared their stories with you, and you believe they have so much inner strength? Do you admire these people and sometimes wish you were like them?

The good news is that you can be just like them and even better. Inner strength is something that can be built up over time and acquired just like any other skill. As a matter of fact, most people are not born with inner strength; they developed it over time. Inner strength is made up of five major components which are, self-discipline, willpower, ability to concentrate, persistence and peace of mind.

These are skills that are essential ingredients for success in any area of your life and they can be learned. However, only a few people are actually willing to deliberately develop these skills and strengthen them with practice. Are you one of them?

If yes, then we are off to a great start. On the other hand, if your answer is no, then I would advise you to start again and I am confident that you will eventually see a need to develop your inner strength.

There are very efficient and effective methods that you can use to develop your inner strength and they revolve around self-denial and deliberate actions. Generally, you can build up your inner strength by becoming more focused on healthy habits and desires, choosing not to satisfy irrelevant and unimportant wants and needs. You can also achieve this by overcoming your inner resistance to do certain things which may appear inconvenient, but which are very relevant to your development.

One of the strategies that you can use is to refrain from negative actions and reactions, while remaining focused on those things that build you up. In the same vein, you should stop satisfying irrelevant desires and change your harmful habits.

Developing your inner strength is really similar to building physical muscles through exercise; you need to practice constantly in order to make yourself stronger and better.

Your inner Venus Warrior is your inner strength, your courage, your belief. She's you, the strong one, the one who always has your back, and the warrior that sticks with you no matter what. The one who tells you, "Yes you can do it. No one can stop you. You've always been great at that!"

That is your inner Venus Warrior.

She has always been there since you were born. She was the one you played games and imagined with when you were young. She is the one who ran with you through the grass barefoot and squealed with joy in the summertime. She is the one who was with you when you battled your enemies in your mind. She has always been with you. But we sometimes lose her.

It is important that you find her again and embrace her; this is the key to unlocking all of your potential and being set firmly on the path to achieving your life's goals and fulfilling your mission. Not only will you have a deeper meaning of life, but you'll be able to make a bigger impact in the world and fulfill that burning desire within you to live your purpose.

In order to fully harness the power of your inner strength, you will need to do a lot of introspection and silent reflection. You will have to get to a point where you can become fully aware of everything that is happening to you and you can currently identify the reason behind each incidence.

Some years ago, I was dating a man for several years and I was deeply in love with him and even had plans for something more than just dating; we had been together for 5 years. We came to a point where we had to make decisions, and instead of staying and working things out, he walked out on the relationship. It was one of the most difficult experiences I have had to deal with; I shut down and it took a lot of work to get over it and begin to live my life again. I moved through all the stages of grief and even gained a lot of weight in the process. However, after a while, I experienced a mind shift and came to the realization that I was not a victim and so should not act like one. It was a life-changing moment for me and my inner Venus Warrior, my personal superhero kicked in.

She exemplifies strength, a loving heart, determination, grit, and a dash of "badass." And she had a habit of showing up at the right moment. I was able to tap into my inner strength, regained my perspective and I realigned my purpose. I realized that I did not like the way I looked and so I lost the weight, became a fitness expert and even went on to compete in physical fitness competitions. I became exceptional at anything I dedicated my time and energy to, and from that moment I understood that I really could not afford to stray far away from my inner Venus Warrior. I made it a point of duty to always connect with her and now, I am on a transformative and deeply insightful path.

What is your inner Venus Warrior saying to you? Can you hear her at all, or has she been silent all the time?

The truth is that whatever we feed our minds with whether consciously or subconsciously will have a direct impact on how we view the world, how we relate with people and even how we relate with ourselves. If our minds are not strong enough, we will just be moving through life without actualizing any of our potential.

Daily Inner Strength Practice

We all have had experiences that challenged us and maybe left us feeling powerless and weak. But, we can turn things around and build up our inner strength so we can feel empowered and ready to take life on.

Try this Daily Inner strength practice to feel more powerful in all areas of your life:

1. Close your eyes and pay attention to your breathing pattern and how you feel in your body.

2. Take a deep breath for 1-5 minutes and repeat it until you feel yourself relax. Make sure the breath comes from your belly.
3. Imagine your breath flowing through the different parts of your body, from the top of your head to the soles of your feet. Picture it like a connection between the different parts of your body.
4. Think back to a time over the past few days that you felt powerless and it seemed like you lacked inner strength.
5. Do a mental scan of your body right now and take note of where you feel any sort of tension in your body. Allow whatever tension you feel to wash over you and dissipate slowly.

6. Identify the emotions you are feeling at the moment. Is it anger, fear, confusion or regret? Allow the emotions to flow through you.
7. What are you currently saying to yourself? What story are you telling yourself about the incident?
8. Ask yourself this, "how old is the part of me that is currently experiencing the story I'm telling?"
9. Let go of the thought and story by saying, "I let this thought go". Say it with conviction and let it go so you are no longer bound by it.
10. Open your eyes and shake the feeling off. Move your body and shake a little to symbolize you letting go of any remnants of unpleasant emotions.

11. Do a mental checklist of your strengths, skills and talents. Also take stock of all the great things you have achieved over the years. Can you feel the good vibes coursing through your veins? How do you feel right now? Strong? Powerful?

You should make it a point to come back to this feeling throughout the day. Repeat this exercise as many times as possible and soon, you will witness a change within you.

The point of this exercise is to remind you that even when things don't go the way you imagined, you do not have to feel weighed down by that. You have the power to determine your reactions and by choosing to let the negative feelings go, you will be increasing your inner strength and preparing yourself for the future.

CHAPTER TWO: CARPE DIEM: RIGHT WHERE YOU ARE

My life began to change when I discovered my Venus Warrior and I was driven to write this book as a result of my experiences and also because my purpose in life is to help women. Having said this, there are only two possible outcomes when you read this book: either it works for you or it does not.

If you do not believe that your inner Venus Warrior exists and you can find her, then this book will not work for you. Or, if you have doubts about your ability to achieve anything you want, then you should probably stop reading this book because the principles shared in here will not work for you.

On the other hand, if you do believe and have seen that you have used your inner Venus Warrior and you have achieved something you strived for in the past, then please continue reading because this book will help you get her back and bring her back into your life.

Ultimately, the outcome depends on you; it all comes down to your mindset. So, what do you believe?

I have coached plenty of women who wanted to find their passion and fulfill their life's purpose. And they've always fallen into two camps: 'the Believers' and 'the Naysayers'.

The believers are the ones that say, "Yes, I can see that this will work for me I know that you can help me, and I believe in myself!" These women have amazing results. The Naysayers on the other hand, are those who say "There's no way that this will work for me, I've always been this way and nothing will ever change," "It's just not possible for me to actually go after what I truly want in my life, how I want to live my life and do what I really want to do." And they are usually right, they never achieve anything at the end of the day. The reason is not far-fetched; those women do not even attempt to gain results and so they remain stuck at the same point.

You may be thinking that I am special because I was able to overcome my own fears and limitations, but I am not. I am just like you. We are one and the same we want to be more, we are tired of the normal and want to live a life that is more than what everyone sees; we are not just enough, we are more than enough. So, even though we have different heights, body sizes, shape, hair color and eye color, there really isn't any major difference between us. You can achieve the same things I have achieved and even more. You also have your inner Venus Warrior and you are about to help her gain expression.

HOW DO YOU START THE PROCESS OF EMBRACING YOURSELF AND REVEALING YOUR VENUS WARRIOR?

How often do you think about who you used to be, who you are now and who you can become some day?

There is no right, or wrong answer and it's okay if you have not given it much thought before, you can start now. However, keep in mind that the process of embracing your Venus Warrior is something that happens right now. So, if you are someone to spend a lot of time thinking about who you used to be, you will need to shift your focus to what is happening now, in the present. This is one of the ways to embrace who you are, understand the present state of your mind and figure out the best way for your inner Venus Warrior to gain expression.

Instead of spending a lot of time worrying about what the future holds or what might happen, how people and events could affect your life, you need to stay focused on how you can make your own changes and experience the process.

There are three major processes through which you can begin the process of unearthing your Venus Warrior. These processes are explained, and I hope you will be able to apply them to your life without holding back.

GAIN FOCUS.

One of the worst things to do to your dreams is to want to do so many things at the same time without any plan in place. It is important that you stay focused on a particular goal and then give it what it takes. Pay close attention to what is going on in your mind as you read these words; what is that one thing that comes to mind? Your mind is feeling a subtle but great shift and when you focus on that one thing, you are effectively channeling all your energy towards making it work.

REVIEW YOUR PERCEPTION.

How do you view the world? How do you see yourself in the world? Are you aware that how you choose to view the world and your role in it influences the course of your life? If you view yourself as a tiny part of the world without anything to contribute, then it is hardly surprising that your Venus Warrior has taken a back seat and has gone into hibernation. Warriors want to fight! So, it is time to review your perception in a way that you shift your attention to things that matter, and the world will start seeing you the way you see yourself. Then, if you want to be a change agent, it is time for you to start seeing yourself as one and ensure that the world sees you that way.

ALIGN YOUR DESIRE.

It is not enough to just gain focus and review your perception of the world and your role in it, you must align all of these with who you currently are. This will allow you to identify areas that need to be fixed so that you can become who you truly want to be. Then, you can make informed decisions without any bias. You need to stay grounded and stay aligned with your goals in order to become who you have dreamt that you can be.

The human mind is naturally conditioned to resist change, so you will have to overcome the resistance and launch yourself into a new reality. The process of becoming reacquainted with your Venus Warrior is a long process and will require a lot of deliberate efforts that sometimes may not be convenient.

I remember sometimes in the course of my own journey that the only thing that kept me going was keeping things simple. I focused on what I wanted the most and worked towards becoming that person; it did not happen overnight, but gradually, things naturally fell into place and I started living the life I wanted.

There'll be times when you will feel discouraged and you will be tempted to bring up arguments about why things will not work out for you. It will be a full-time job to counter such thoughts and focus on your strengths. You will have to do this as many times as is required until it becomes second nature to have only words of encouragement for yourself.

Looking back at my own experience and those of the women I have coached, I can state positively that there is a group of women who try so hard to prove themselves. They chase after accomplishments and external validation but fail to recognize that all the accolades mean nothing when they still feel empty inside. Sometimes, we are just hiding behind accomplishments and pretending to have it all together until someone finds us and helps us realize that truth about ourselves.

I have discovered that while there is no one-size-fits-all answer to this challenge, a combination of small practices can help you embrace who you are and figure out how to make your Venus Warrior express herself. The following tips have been proven to be helpful and I am sure they will help you too.

Let go of what you cannot control. Identify the things that are within your control and let go of the pressure of trying to fix things that you have no business trying to fix. For instance, you are not responsible for people's happiness. You are responsible for yourself and being a decent person. You do not need the added pressure of trying to be someone else or helping them live their own lives. Also, you cannot control people's opinion about you, so why do you bother? Live life on your terms and stop seeking for external validation.

Challenge your limits. I have learned that facing my fears is a good way to make myself feel stronger. Fear never disappears on its own; you must do something about it and the best thing is to face it head on. So, identify your fears and challenge your limits.

Enjoy the process. It is okay to make mistakes and to not have all the answers. It is equally okay to look silly while trying new things and taking risks to help you develop your confidence. You have to start somewhere even if you suck at it, it sure beats not doing anything. And, like I pointed out earlier, the result is important, but the process is way more important.

Know yourself. This is possibly an understated process; you need to be curious about yourself. Ask yourself probing questions and identify the things that truly matter to you, outside of what other people think. It is okay to be different from other people but still find a way to coexist.

Be vulnerable. This is one of the hardest things I have had to do. Everyone has this image of a strong woman who has it all together and should not break down for whatever reason. It is important that you have someone that you can be vulnerable with; it could be a best friend, a partner, a parent or a mentor. This ensures that you have a good support system in place to help you through life.

Allow yourself to feel. It is not wrong to be emotional; being strong or being a warrior does not mean you have to appear strong all the time. You should avoid burying your feelings; express yourself and allow yourself to become more familiar with your internal dialogue and processes.

Have fun. You don't have to work hard all the time. Make sure you take some time to relax, do the things you enjoy and connect with your family, friends and colleagues.

These tips are not exhaustive and are only pointers to help you see how you can position yourself and prepare for the full expression of your inner Venus Warrior.

We all have our personal journeys, and this is why you must embrace who you are. All your life experiences made you who you are today and brought you to this point where you are ready to hear this message. You are amazing. You have battled wars that no one else has. Life isn't supposed to be easy. It's supposed to challenge us so that we can grow and develop and change!

So, this is my challenge to you. This book will challenge you to think differently. It will challenge you to stop living in the past. To stop thinking of all the negativity, self-doubt, and no confidence. When these emotions start to happen, push them away. Don't quit on yourself. You've got this! I know it. Because I've done it too.

When you do hit resistance and you want to push the book aside and you don't want to believe anything in it, do yourself the greatest thing that you can do. Ask yourself this:

"Is it possible?"

"Can I truly believe what I've always wanted to be?"

"Is it possible that I can go after my dreams and finally live the life that I want?"

If you do this, I promise you that you will be a different person by the end of this book.

CHAPTER THREE: THE PAST IS JUST THAT

The past is just that, the past. It may have made you who you are today, but it should not hold so much power over you that it makes you doubt yourself today. But the truth is that you are not a product of your past, rather you are a product of your actions.

We have all experienced hurt in one way or another. And as you have probably discovered, sometimes the memories that you do not want to have are the ones that always seem to find a way to keep coming back. It would seem like these memories have a mind of their own and each time they evoke very strong reactions from you. Over time, you discover that you are becoming limited in varying aspects of your life ranging from relationships to work, studies and even your career and family. You start having a stunted view of life tainted with neediness and distrust.

The truth is that what you choose to do with the hurt is inarguably more important than the hurt in itself. Would you prefer to be bound by the hurt in your past, wasting quality time thinking about it and crying over something that cannot be changed? Or would you rather rise above your hurt, get back on your feet and give life what it takes?

I have been in this situation where the hurt from my past threatened to take over my life and shut down my inner warrior forever. The hurt was debilitating and instead of getting better, the more I whined about them, the worse things got. For example, I was extremely bullied as a child in school. I was just different, and I had very little to no self-worth—no self-confidence.

I didn't quite understand why I was bullied. I remember my first day of kindergarten. I didn't speak much English since Portuguese is my first language. I remember standing in the school yard with the other kids circled around me and their voices sounded like the teacher in Charlie Brown. I was so frustrated by the end of the day that I bit the interior vinyl of my Mom's Dodge Aspen car door when she picked me up. I saw those teeth marks for 10 years. They haunted me every day and reminded me of my insecurities.

I recall being under so much pressure when I was transitioning from high school to college. It resulted in my gaining so much weight that I weighed 215 pounds! I did not even realize this was happening until I had gained the weight and had to begin the process of getting it off. It was a rough time of my life. Additionally, I used to be quite athletic in high school, so just imagine dealing with the new reality that I weighed that much. The more I thought about it, the more incapacitated I felt.

There was another major curveball in my life; my boyfriend of over five years broke up with me. Yes, you guessed right, I was devastated and in no time, I put a lot of the weight that I had tried to lose back on. It was a difficult time for me, and it took everything I had in me to avoid getting swept away by the wave of depression. I had moments when I wondered if I was not good enough or if something was fundamentally wrong with me that made people reject me. It took a while, a long while, but I eventually sorted through my feelings, my reactions and I became stronger for it.

One thing I tried to avoid completely was blaming other people for the things that were happening to me. While it is true that people did things to hurt me, they did not have any power to determine how I would react to the things they did. Usually, we want people to admit they hurt us, and we want them to take steps towards amends or a sincere apology at the very least. The downside with having reactions that are based on other people's actions is that you cannot control other people or make them act in a certain way.

If someone hurt you and you want to wait for them to apologize to you before you feel better, you may be stuck there for a very, very long time. At the end of the day, you will end up feeling worse than if you had found a way to resolve the hurt on your own.

It is important that you know that your feelings and emotional responses are valid, and you are allowed to explore them to the fullest. But you need to move on after a while. You need to take back your power and ensure that you do not hold on to past hurt so much that you get stuck in limbo, neither making progress or moving on.

DO NOT GIVE YOUR PAST SO MUCH POWER!

The only way to be truly free of past hurt, is to consciously create a space in your mind to settle things and let go. This is guaranteed to make sure you have the full freedom to enjoy your present without being weighed down by the past. How do you ensure that you do not give your past so much power over your present realities?

First, you must make a conscious decision to let go. This is possibly the most difficult step and the most important; anything different from this simply means you are setting yourself up to fail. It is wishful thinking to expect that things will disappear on their own or that "time heals every wound." You would be surprised at how much hurt doesn't get resolved just by the passing of time. You need to *choose* to let it go, to stop dwelling on the pain and to live without that particular hurt.

Second, if you feel like expressing how you feel about the incidence, then you should do it. For some people, they look for a means to vent either to a friend, a confidant or a mentor while some people prefer to write in a journal or to scream into a large empty space. Whatever means you choose; the important thing is to express how you feel. Afterwards, you need to accept responsibility for the role you played in getting to that point. It does not matter if you played a huge role or a minor role, this step is important when reviewing events and trying to figure out how you would react to a similar situation in the future. You need to decide what you will do; will you remain a helpless victim, or will you take a proactive step to get over the hurt?

Then, you need to erase the "victim mentality" and get over yourself. The more you blame other people for what happened to you, the more difficult it would be to get over it and move on. You need to get to a point where you take responsibility for your happiness and completely sever any ties that your state of mind has with an event from your past. Devote your energy to being a better person. Trust me, it took me a long time to accomplish this one.

It is equally important that you focus more on your present and be determined to enjoy life to the fullest. Ignore every tendency to slip into "victim mode" and keep telling stories about how you were hurt; instead choose to talk about your growth and how you were able to overcome the pain in your past! Spend more of your time celebrating your victories than crying over past hurt and pain; you'll be surprised at how much things will change in a little while.

I'd like to clarify that these steps are very invasive and will require that you are brutally honest with yourself. I am not talking about putting a Band-Aid on the places that hurt, rather, I am talking about complete and wholesome healing. This is the only way to ensure that you are ready to meet your inner Venus Warrior and not a pseudo-warrior who hasn't gotten over their past.

Above all else, you must learn to forgive yourself and the people that hurt you.

Forgiveness gives you a new lease on life, it gives you so much freedom and when done sincerely, you will feel lighter in your mind, body and soul. When you forgive someone, it means you are truly ready to let the past go and move on with your life. It also means that you have picked up valuable lessons from the event and gradually, you are becoming a better person for it.

The ultimate freedom from the past is achieved when you can honestly define yourself outside of your past. This means you must find out who you are and be ready to embrace what you find. This is what it means to find your inner Venus Warrior- your true identity when all the façade is lifted.

You may be tempted to believe that who you are is a result of the things that happened to you; but what if I told you that you are way more than that? You are not the sum of your emotions, thoughts or experiences; they are a part of you, but they are not you. YOU ARE MORE and you need to find out who you are.

Who I Am Now and How Did I Discover This?

If you're like me, you probably have found that when you reach that next thing, there's no celebration. There's not even any joy in it because we find ourselves pushing and pushing for things that are not in alignment with who we truly are. You may know me as the overachiever, the woman who has three Bachelor's degrees in science, Dual Master's in science, an MBA and is successful all around on the outside; the big house, the kids, the husband, the career, everything.

Having everything doesn't necessarily mean we are fulfilled on the inside.

To anyone looking from the outside, I had everything. But did I really have everything? I had a serious case of inferiority complex and lack of self-confidence, and they could be traced to my lack of self-worth. There is no denying that if you have little or no self-worth, you would have zero self-confidence.

Having a healthy sense of self-worth means you value yourself. Having a sense of self-value means that you are worthy. Self-worth is defined by Merriam-Webster as: "a feeling that you are a good person who deserves to be treated with respect."

I knew I was a good person. I pushed through. I had friends that never left my side. They are the ones that I put my love and trust into. That feeling of happiness and love is what helped me get through the hard times. I needed to focus on the good and not on the bad. I had to let myself feel the emotion of happiness and get through the sadness. I would imagine being on top of the world and that nothing would hurt me. I did a lot of imagining. And it helped. For a bit. But my Venus Warrior was battling every day against the sharp words and actions of the bullies. She was wounded quite often.

It was when I realized as a little girl while sitting in the bathroom at thirteen trying to take my own life, that I understood that my thoughts were what was making the difference. I realized that what I was saying to myself in the conversation in my head was a completely separate entity from who I actually was. That voice inside of me was almost like a third person had joined the conversation. It didn't feel like me talking anymore. It was then that I had a small glimmer of hope that maybe I could change it all.

I had a lot of struggles, ups, and downs, all throughout my life but I still had the hope in knowing that I could change it if I would just believe in my inner strength. It came from a lot of pretending. Lots and lots of acting as what I wanted to be. Almost as if I was fooling myself but with the years of fooling myself, I finally came to believe that I was that person I was pretending to be.

Over time, I got stronger by being deliberate with my choices and moving even when all I wanted to do was to just lie down and just watch time pass. I hit a lot of rough patches on my way; going from high school to college was a struggle. I knew no one and I started from scratch again. This is when my weight started to climb on. Eventually, I didn't recognize myself anymore after ballooning up to 215 pounds. I was an athlete in high school and yet I was doing nothing now. That woman that I was starting to turn into from the pretending vanished as quickly as it appeared. The same thing happened when I was dumped by my five-year long-term boyfriend. I didn't fit into any of my clothing, not even my boyfriend's extra-large shorts. I knew that I had to get myself out of this hole. I knew I would be able to do it again. So, I had to start all over again. Little by little I did the pretending again, and little by little I saw myself as what I wanted to be, and little by little I climbed out of that hole and became who I was internally. I still forgot that my inner Venus Warrior was waiting for me to be released.

I pulled and pulled, and I knew that I would thrive. I threw myself into my studies, finishing three Bachelor of Science degrees. I wanted to be a veterinarian and I had the aspiration to go on into the medical field, but I was waitlisted. Feeling as though I went through a "quarter-life crisis" I didn't know what I was going to do but I was determined to keep forging ahead. I had an idea that I could do better, and I was determined to not let that dream die.

I decided to pursue my research and earn a Dual Master's in Molecular Biology and Microbiology. I felt as though I could cure the world. I knew what it was like to be strong I knew what it took to get out of that deep dark place, and I knew how to help women do the same. I was always coaching and helping women all along my journey, and everything that I went through, I would use to help others. I would empower women and make sure they knew that they could also achieve whatever it is that they wanted in their lives. I was doing empowerment before empowerment was a thing. Just like selfies, I was always taking selfies in the 90s before selfies were even a thing.

At first, my achievements were all these degrees, but I was still not happy. I knew I could do better. So, I threw myself into fitness competitions to change how I felt about how I looked. I was determined to become fit again and I gave it all it required. I competed for four years and with my massive weight loss journey and getting on stage and competing for a fitness competition, I helped others do the same. I inspired people with my weight loss journey and commitment to achieving my goal.

Moving on, I climbed the corporate ladder moving quickly from bench scientist to field scientist, to consulting. It was not a rosy journey and at some point, I felt like I was losing myself again. But this time I took active steps to ensure that I did not get blindsided; I was ready to face all of the setbacks and challenges. I had discovered my inner Venus Warrior and we were ready to take anything life threw at us. I was a super strong and independent woman who had learned how to get through rocks and hard places. I learned how to achieve things, overcome challenges and come out of that dark hole and also help others to do the same.

I discovered truths about myself, embraced who I was and got comfortable in my own skin. Today, I can confidently say that I am ready for anything that life may throw at me; I have built up my defenses and will not back down for any reason.

BENEFITS OF KNOWING WHO YOU ARE

In addition to being a prerequisite to discovering your Venus Warrior, here are some more benefits of knowing who you are.

Be your own expert. This means that you have a full understanding of what makes you tick. You do not need to go through the trials and errors every time; you will be able to identify situations that will help you grow way ahead of time and you'll be able to identify toxic situations as well. Above all, you won't need anyone to tell you how to react in specific situations. You will be in charge of your own life.

Be self-reliant and be your own best friend. This means that you will learn to put yourself first, protect your space and identify what works for you. You will accept yourself just like a best friend who knows all your weaknesses bust still sticks with you regardless. You will also learn to be less strict or critical of yourself, and begin to treat yourself with more kindness.

Be original and get rid of inferiority complex. When you know who you are, you will not see any need to compare yourself with other people. You will be your own true self and less easily influenced by other people. Also, you will stop living in fear of not matching up or not being good enough.

Learn to take risks and eliminate regrets. You'll get rid of the self-doubt and several questions that keep you from trying new things. You will also stop over-analyzing and negative thinking. You will become more comfortable with the fact that it is okay to win and to lose sometimes, because those things do not define you.

Be present and available in relationships. The quality of your relationships will improve because you will know what drives you and you can easily tell when a relationship will be beneficial to you or not.

And you will know what you deserve and will not settle for less.

The benefits of knowing yourself cannot be overemphasized; you will be able to focus more on the things that matter, making it easier for you to identify your passion and discover your purpose. In no time, things will begin to fall into place for you and those dreams that appeared vague will appear even more real.

So, regardless of the events that happened to you in your past, you can create the kind of present you want for yourself. It is time you gave your inner Venus Warrior a chance. It's been long enough.

CHAPTER FOUR: PHOENIX HOUR

The phoenix is a bird in Greek mythology with the ability to recreate itself, which means that it never dies. It goes through an eternal cycle and when it is time for the end of its present life, it settles into a nest and burns to ashes. And then it rises from the ashes as a renewed bird. Some believe that the Phoenix is able to see when its end is approaching, so it knows what it must do and it goes ahead to do it while bearing the end in mind- the chance to become something more than it used to be. In essence, in order to become more than you used to be, you have to start with the end in mind, believing that you have the ability to break down everything you have ever known and rise from the ruins as a better version of ourselves. This is the Phoenix hour.

The journey to finding your inner Venus Warrior demands that you face your deepest fears; it is a journey of in-depth exploration that requires you to accept that you may need to change everything you used to think you know. And, you have to be ready to be broken and then pieced back together again. There is a tendency that your mind will try to convince you to take a seemingly faster and less painful route, so you must be determined to stay true to yourself and the process.

You can think of this process as a sort of spiritual awakening that results in a mind shift which will be responsible for the growth you will definitely experience. This process starts from the initial realization of the depth of your pain or disillusionment. For most people, the initial feeling is a sort of darkness and emptiness as a result of coming face to face with their pain and inadequacies for the very first time. However, when you can face it without wavering, you begin to experience real growth. Your level of self-awareness increases, and you will be poised to enter into the life you have always envisioned for yourself.

When you are able to go through the darkness and come out at the other end of the tunnel, your eyes will be open to new horizons and the possibilities that lie ahead of you will be expanded even more. It is important that you do not try to rush into anything after your phoenix hour; this will ensure that you do not get wounded again and become frustrated. However, if you do get clarity in your mind and are prompted to do something, then you should go ahead and get it done.

I went through my phoenix hour several times before I realized what was happening, but as soon as I did, I embraced the process and this launched me into a new level where I was not only reborn, but I also became a voice to guide other people through their own process. It is important that you realize that each person's journey is unique, and you may never find someone with the same story as yours. However, what matters is that you keep moving and never lose sight of the end goal- to be more.

I remember clearly on the third day of being home with my son and breastfeeding that I felt that my world had completely collapsed. I felt as if though I lost myself and that I would never ever be the same woman again. I felt hopeless, I felt as though my identity was completely gone. I will never be the same person again. I thought that I lost all my independence and then the sadness crept in. Feeling as though everything I worked so hard for in the past 30 years was completely gone. I love my son, I would have done anything for him, but I felt as though life would never be the same and not for the better.

I went through life raising my son and trying over and over to be the best mommy, the best career woman, the best wife. I then had my second child, my daughter, and even though it has been two years, I felt that I was almost back to who I was, and it all started all over again. My daughter was way fussier than my son, both who never slept through the night, both who had colic and acid reflux, and in dealing with all of that, I lost myself again.

It was when I turned 40 that the clarity finally hit. There had to be more to my life than just striving, pushing, achieving goals and climbing one corporate ladder after another. Is this really it? Is this what life is meant to be? Have you ever felt anything like that? Women ask me for help and ask how I got to where I am today. They are all hoping, searching and wishing that something would change, something would give, but for some reason things never seem to work out. I knew that what I had been doing the last two decades wasn't in alignment with who I really was, but I had to get to a point where I couldn't take it anymore before I decided to pursue my true passion. You do not have to wait for two decades to find out what your passion is; if you listen closely to your inner dialogue, you will be able to tell if what you are doing does not align with your purpose. When you have it figured out, you'll be surprised that it took you that long, because it has probably been staring you in the face all along.

My life's passion is to help women discover themselves just like I did, and this is why I have to share my story now, because I do not want you to lose two decades of your life as I did. Not only that, but I want you to know you have the power and the empowerment necessary to actually go after what you want and you can achieve anything that you want—no matter what you've been through.

Today, I am a transformation and empowerment coach. I've spent years developing ways to help women find fulfillment, and I coach women to find the power they hold inside of them. What this will do for me is allow me to leave the corporate ladder I couldn't get off of, and I will have time freedom that allows me to drop my kids off at school, take coaching calls, teach empowerment programs, chaperone my kids field trips, spend time with my best friend—my husband—and I'll be able to take trips with my family, attend conferences and events, take care of my elderly parents and not feel one ounce of guilt about how I show up in the world today. My life is beautiful because I found the power within me to recognize my worth, know my strength, and find my path and purpose. My inner Venus Warrior was just waiting to be set free!

I was living my life in the corporate world as I mentioned earlier, and it was consuming me. I used to have what I call, "The Sunday Depression". Every single Sunday I would get into this massive sadness around 4:00 in the afternoon every week. It was like, "I have to get up tomorrow and do this five day stretch of miserable work again." Miserable isn't even a strong enough word for it. I'm sure some of you have had that pit in your stomach on Sunday, and you just feel like you can't take another week of the same horrendous routine. It wasn't in alignment with who I am. I always felt like I was supposed to save the world. Like I had this higher purpose and that's why I got into research science. I was working for companies that were trying to cure cancer and were doing stem cell research, and even though those are very noble endeavors, I just didn't feel fulfilled. The only thing that made me happy in those positions was people. Helping people was what made me feel like I was doing something right. I just wanted to help people change their outlook, to help them change their perspective and live a fulfilling and happy life. It was a dark time in my life when I was trying to find my place.

One thing that I realized was that going through hard times in school, it really taught me that I could achieve anything I wanted to. Going back to when I was 13 and wanted to take my own life, there was a minute, a vision, that told me that it was something I could get past. I could achieve happiness, I could do good in the world, and I could change so much if I really wanted to. I just had to build what I call my inner Venus Warrior. That's what I want for you. I want you to build your inner Venus Warrior. I'm here to help you achieve it.

Maximizing the Phoenix Hour

No one is immune from challenges, crisis or adversity in any form. Yet, rather than bow under the pressure of such challenges, you should use them as a springboard to your next level! One of the most common misconceptions about handling crisis is that you are preparing for something that may never actually happen. What you should be doing is accepting the power that you have and then taking full control of your life.

When you are in control, every potential meltdown or challenging situation is viewed as a Phoenix hour and you must be prepared to handle it as such.

In order to do this effectively, you have to take responsibility for the choices you will make which even if they will not immediately change your circumstance, will effectively determine the outcome and of course it will influence your reaction and how you choose to experience it.

You should view every Phoenix hour as a blessing and here are some steps that you can use to maximize the process.

STEP 1: FACE REALITY

There is absolutely no need to hide your feelings or attempt to sugarcoat the situation; you should face reality and analyze the situation honestly and with a sense of duty. It is best that you recognize what the challenges are, accept the reality and allow yourself to express all the feelings you have at that point; it could be hurt, disappointment, anger, confusion, pain or even happiness. Whatever you feel is valid and will serve as pointers to help you decide the course of action to take.

STEP 2: TAKE ACTION

Although it may seem like an intimidating task to start mapping out the rest of your future at this point, evaluating the circumstances and identifying areas where small steps would make a huge difference will help you build up your confidence level. This is the point during which you should keep your mind open for the different possibilities that will present themselves to you and then find the ones that fit into your passion. It might be tempting to want to stick to familiar territory only, but you have to spread your wings and explore other options.

STEP 3: AVOID SELF-BLAME

It is human nature to want to blame yourself for making wrong decisions over the years or not being strong enough when it was needed. Regardless of the decisions you have made, you should avoid blaming yourself because you can easily get overwhelmed with the unpleasant emotions which will make it difficult to stay focused on the end goal. Avoid slipping into a pattern of self-pity, instead place more emphasis on what you need to do. Choose to rise above all of it!

STEP 4: HAVE A SUPPORT SYSTEM

This means you do not have to go through the process alone. You should share your journey with people who are close to you; please share with people that will give you honest and helpful advice and not people who will mock your journey. In a situation where you are not sure of who you can speak with, you can keep a journal or talk to a professional. This is where I come in, my goal is to help you get empowered and to walk with you through the process of becoming more than what you used to be.

STEP 5: PRIORITIZE SELF-CARE

The importance of this cannot be over-emphasized; you need to engage in rewarding activities, have healthy habits and guarantee you take care of your body. You should spend some quality time doing things you love, relax and just focus on taking good care of yourself. Avoid wasting time on mental arguments about what could have been, what you could have done differently and so on. Focus on you in the now.

STEP 6: LEARN YOUR LESSONS

Every event and the accompanying process has lessons that serve as an opportunity for growth. Take some time out to identify the lessons in each situation, know what you could have done differently, learn what you should keep doing and know how to avoid future recurrence if that's what applies.

STEP 7: LEARN TO TRUST AGAIN

This is arguably one of the most difficult parts of this process, is trusting yourself to not "mess things up" again and learning to trust people not to hurt you or make you revisit your past. However, this is a very important step in the process and if you want to maximize it, you will need to trust again. It may take some time, but you will realize that life is a lot better when there is love and trust.

These steps are not necessarily time-bound, so take as much time as you need in order to be fully ready to launch into life again. It is <u>your</u> Phoenix hour and your Venus Warrior is within you to help you make the best of it.

The phoenix signifies a lot of things which includes hope, renewal, and rebirth. The phoenix is very similar to my story and this is why I have shared the story with you. I was presented with very challenging situations, even up to the point of almost taking my own life. But I was able to overcome all of that and just like the phoenix, I came out renewed from the ashes of my experiences. The same thing can happen to you too and here are some lessons you can learn from my experience.

Life will take its natural course

You have little control over certain episodes that happen to you in life, but you have maximum control over your reaction. The best thing you can do is to ride the waves and enjoy the process. I promise the end result is worth it.

Resistance is natural

Stop trying so hard to keep things the way they used to be; allow the change to take its course and welcome it. Embrace the chaos when it comes but ensure you stand firm in what you believe in. Give room for the fire to burn down your defenses and expose your weaknesses to its cleansing power. Allow yourself to burn like the phoenix and then look forward to your rebirth and renewal.

Focus on the positive things

There will be dark moments when it would seem like you have more reasons to be sad than happy. You might even begin to lose interest in the things that used to give you joy. In times like that, you must take conscious steps to remember the good times. You need to be intentional about the things you do; hang out with friends and take part in activities that you enjoy.

Stay focused

Rather than focus on the bigger picture that may appear too abstract, you can take things a day at a time. Each step in your journey will lead you to the next and at your own pace. The phoenix already knows what comes next, so it submits itself to every step of the process without rushing. So, pay attention and celebrate your little victories.

The resilience of your mind

Regardless of what you may be going through, you will eventually find wholeness.

The human mind is resilient and with proper guidance, will find its way home. It took a while, but I found my way and I am sure you will find yours too.

Judging from my experience and the experience of the people I have worked with, discovering your inner Venus Warrior is a highly deliberate process that will require you to:

- Give up trying to control everything
- Accept you don't know everything
- Let things take their natural course
- Stay focused
- Enjoy the process
- Celebrate your little victories
- Learn the lessons

The image of the phoenix rising from the ashes is quite powerful and is symbolic for how your suppressed Venus Warrior will rise after you have gone through the process of becoming more.

Life could be tricky, presenting you with contrasting experiences intertwined with each other; happiness and pain, excitement and boredom, and so on. You cannot pick and choose; you must experience it all in your everyday life. But the truth is that you can rise above it and you will!

Avoid becoming numb to everything going around you, even if the process is super painful and takes a lot of time, the end will justify the means. You are a phoenix waiting to rise from the ashes with your Venus Warrior at the forefront. It is a time for you to be healed, restored, and revived.

This is the time to decide what you want: Do you want to get burned and come out renewed or do you want to remain "safe" in your comfort zone?

CHAPTER FIVE: END THE BULLSHIT:

WHAT'S YOUR PLAN?

We talked about the benefits of embracing your inner Venus Warrior. But, there's the question of how you do that consistently without wavering. You need to have a plan that details your action steps based on your vision and what drives you. This is the only way to ensure that you will not get caught up with the "I am enough" narrative anymore; now you will be set to become more, and you can inspire other people to be more.

In my journey, my vision was what my driving force was. I had to clearly envision myself the way I wanted my life and in detail.

It wasn't just "I want to have money," I had to lay out every detail of what my ideal life looked like. I wanted to be a best-selling author, so I had to ask myself, "What does a best-selling author do?" A best-selling author spreads their message by seeing it vividly. I like to use the word pretend, to pretend to be that person you allow yourself to really begin to feel inside what it feels like to be that person. This helps you get in alignment and to see yourself as you see who you really truly are. Life tends to fall apart when we're putting all our effort after somebody else's definition of success. When we don't value our values, that's when the collapse comes.

You've spent all these years working so hard to achieve something and to make your life great. You know what you want to do. You have that burning desire to be happy in your life and to fight for what you want, but life happened to you too. You've got married, had kids, and got the house and the debt, and that Venus Warrior inside you was quiet. You love your family. I have no question about that. But most of your outside life has nothing to do with who you truly are on the inside.

Know that you have the courage to find and make the changes so that you can move your life from the life that you currently have to a life that is going to be fulfilling for you and who you are supposed to be.

As I said, best-selling authors go on book tours, they go to speaking events, and they spread their message. I had to actually envision myself going on book tours, speaking at events, spreading my message. To give the power back to my inner Venus Warrior, I had to dig deep inside to find the courage that I had muffled. Use the voice you have inside of you to speak your aligned life into existence!

So, you might be asking, "What does a Venus Warrior look like?" Imagine a woman who has, in her life, always worked for whatever it was that she wanted. She always achieved it. She's young, and she knew she could do great things, and she did. She had a fight inside of her. Then she gains a career, got married and had kids, and then the house and the debt, and what happens is she is quieted, she is suffocated. She wakes up and her heart sinks because she knows that this is the life she has created. One day, the woman decides, "enough is enough" and she has reached her breaking point. She knows she isn't living her best life, and she isn't servicing anyone, including herself, so she knows she has to change. The courage to seek help, to search and figure it out hits her and she begins the process of figuring out what will fulfill her. Maybe she adopts a child, maybe she loses 30 pounds. Maybe she changes careers, maybe she gets a promotion. Whatever it is, it doesn't have to be this massive thing, it just has to be something that makes her truly happy and it trickles into everything else in her life. Once she is fulfilled on the inside, everything around them changes. She has awakened her inner Venus Warrior.

Letting those circumstances get in the way, letting our limiting beliefs stop us from becoming everything we were meant to become is what puts us in this state. We don't know where or how to start, we don't know what the journey looks like or entails, and so we put it off, we make excuses, and we stop ourselves from achieving our dreams. The thing is, these changes don't have to be drastic. You don't have to flip your entire world upside down. One thing at a time. What is one thing that you want to change right now? Start there. Envision yourself after the change. What does that look like? Be detailed in your answer, that's how you make the change.

It's so easy to make excuses. We all have circumstances in our life that get in the way of being the best version of ourselves. We say, "I can't because..." and then there's a whole list of reasons and they're all legitimate. But these things are all things that are limiting beliefs. They're allowing you to give in to the fear and they're all based in the back that you've stopped realizing who you are, you've given in to the circumstances and you're now living paralyzed without having any thoughts about how to even start. There's just too much going on in your life and around you, and you have given yourself responsibility, even for things that don't belong to you or should not be in your awareness, and now something drastic has to be done to relieve some of the pressure and get you back on track.

If I had known what my life would be like, I would have done this way earlier than this. I would have taken charge of my life and would have been more careful about the things I allowed to influence my state of mind and eventually, my outcomes. I wouldn't have let the fear hold me back from moving forward. But here I was, going through the motions and taking on labels like "super mom" but I was miserable on the inside and looking for a way out. If I could do things differently, I wouldn't have missed my daughter's first birthday because I was in a training for my job, I wouldn't have missed our wedding anniversary because of work, and I wouldn't have been constantly stressed out about money. I honestly could have done so many things if I didn't waste two decades of my life doing what pulled me down. But now, I know better and I have made it a mission to share my experiences with other women so they can avoid making the same mistakes that I made.

Here's the thing; you don't have to go all out with a bang neither to have any effect or drastic changes on a large scale. You can start small and then scale up, until you have changed everything that needs to be changed in your life to give room for your new realities. It can be as simple as picking one thing that you want to change and focusing on that, you would have to give it everything it takes and stay committed to seeing the process through to the end.

This is your opportunity to change everything in your life and I hope you grab it with both hands. I'm sure you're like me by this point; you're ready to take action and you're thinking; I wish I could have started so much sooner. I am glad you are ready to do whatever it will take to awaken your Venus Warrior. But first, I want to remind you of some things that you should absolutely avoid doing:

Don't allow the fear of who you've become get in the way!

Don't let that "Supermom" label stop you from being super you!

Don't let everybody else's dreams keep you from fulfilling yours!

The average woman out there is expected to be a lot of things to many people, she is expected to be there for people whenever they need her, and they will need her- a lot. This is why you will need to put yourself first when you want to make these life-changing decisions. It is okay to be "selfish" and put yourself ahead of everyone else this time; go all out for your dreams and do what you have always wanted to do.

If there is anything I could tell you right now—one takeaway—I hope you know yourself better today than you did yesterday.

WHAT DO YOU NEED TO DO?

In the words of Aristotle, "A good life is one where you develop your strengths, realize your potential, and become what it is in your nature to become." Then, we can say the essence of this journey to becoming more is to live a good life. In order to do this, you need to cultivate strengths that make it possible for you to pursue your goals; such strengths include honesty, persistence, loyalty, generosity, and others. You need to be able to identify your strengths and then figure out how to display them in every area of your life.

The areas of your life affected will depend on the roles you play in life; for example, you could be a mother, wife, teacher, sister, daughter, lover, and friend and so on. Make a list of the different roles you play in life and then you can proceed to arrange them in order of priority and how important they are to you. Always bear in mind that you need to take care of yourself too, so you need to be on the list as well!

Thereafter, you have to carry out the following exercises for each role you have listed:

1. Write down your purpose for each role. For example, "as a mother, my role is to take care of my children and raise adults who can change their society for good."

2. Write down the future you want for yourself in that role. This means that you have to visualize yourself in that role in the future and state what you would want your best-case scenario to be like.
3. Write down the current situation of each role. How are you doing? Are you on track to achieving your goals?
4. Write down what you think needs to be done differently to help you achieve your purpose in each role as stated above.
5. Write down an action plan detailing things that you would be doing to help you get to the best case scenario for each role as you stated above. The action plan which should be time

bound and very specific for each stated role.

It is important to know that in order to create a major mind shift; you must write down your plan and how you intend to go through the process. This should be taken in order and could include the following steps:

State your intention clearly

We all have desires, dreams, wishes and memories. Yet, in order to get the best results, you must state your intentions clearly. Here's an example, you should say "I want my finances to improve" rather than "I want my life to change". You need to be specific and precise.

Meditate on your desires and let them mature

This involves you visualizing what you want to achieve and spending a substantial amount of time thinking about them. This is different from fantasizing; it is a whole lot more realistic and you can almost begin to feel the situation unfolding.

Embrace your feelings about your intention

As you meditate and visualize, you should start receiving different feelings about the desired change. Embrace all of it, whether positive or negative and then study your response. Does it feel real or not?

Be willing to let it go

Be ready to let your original plan go depending on how the future unfolds. You do not have to have full control over everything; just allow nature to take its course after you have done your own due diligence. This will help you avoid disappointments when things don't go as you expected.

Break down your resistance to change

This is another important step that needs to be taken seriously. The human mind is naturally tuned to resist change. You have to be ready to fight a battle with your "mind" to get rid of insecurities, anxiety and doubts that may want to hold you back.

Make a plan to overcome obstacles

When making any plan, you have to consider the possible dangers or delays that may come up in the course of your journey. Then make a plan to overcome them; you might consider getting an accountability partner, a mentor or a therapist who can serve as a support system. They will also serve as a sounding board to help fine-tune your ideas.

Be realistic

Avoid being too dreamy with your plans; set goals that are realistic and achievable to you now. If you do not believe them then you will not achieve them. Assess and identify the things you need to change, the things you cannot change yet and the things that you have to get rid of. Make a list of as many items as possible and then proceed to take the action points you've listed. There is no need to rush and you can keep tweaking the list until you come up with something that works.

Start with the little things

Even little successes are still successes! So, begin from the peripheral and work towards the core of the challenges. Tackle the problems you know you can handle first and then continue to the bigger deals. This will help you build up your confidence.

Pay attention to the change happening inside you

Be self-aware all the time. Ensure that you break away from unhealthy habits and take up new roles that will help you remain on the path you have chosen. You may try keeping a detailed journal of your journey as this will help you appreciate your process more in the future.

Stay connected to a higher source of inspiration

Depending on your personal beliefs, you should look up to any higher power that makes you feel safe. It may be through meditation or some other means; whatever it is, you should have a method through which you connect to a higher source. This will further help you in your journey.

These steps have been proven over time to be very effective in connecting with your inner Venus Warrior. I hope you are able to fully utilize them and make the best of the process.

You can make the journey easier for yourself by creating morning rituals that highlight your strengths and will help you develop the desired behavioral changes required to help you achieve your goal. You can start out with the toughest things and then work your way through all of it. This will ensure that you spend your early hours on the things that require more of your energy and willpower.

You should pay attention to everything you are doing and evaluate their effectiveness regularly. This will ensure that you are not just doing this for the sole purpose of doing them, but with the aim of achieving an actual result. This is especially important because sometimes the things you expect to work are not the things working. So, you will have to reevaluate your position and make the necessary adjustments.

If, at any point, it seems like things are getting out of hand, you can switch things up and start with the easiest things. Smashing smaller goals have been proven to help boost the confidence level and will also help you cultivate healthy habits. And, if you feel like you are not making progress, then you can just make it as simple as possible.

Just like I said earlier, the most important thing is the process and what you learn while on the journey. So, if it seems like a big order, simplify it and focus on one thing at a time. Identify one thing that cuts across all the roles that you play in your life and then focus on developing it.

The journey to becoming more than enough never ends and it is quite easy to get lost just trying to figure things out. My approach and the advice I always give the women I have worked with, is to stay focused and take it one day at a time.

You see the one thing that you can never get back is time. I look back across my life, especially in those two decades, and I see all the things that I should have never missed. I don't have any regrets, but I confidently would do some things differently if I were to go back in time. Saying this, I want you to start to daydream, to close your eyes and soak everything in. In the process, you should have a clearer picture of the Venus Warrior that is within you.

It's extremely possible at this stage in your life that it may be just the tiniest flicker, but embrace that flicker, and allow yourself to pretend and really see it. I know that deep within you, you know who you are and what you really want to be. Stop making excuses for why you can't and begin to visualize you living and being that person. Write out what that perfect picture would be.

How visualization works to help you achieve your goals

Before your goal can become real, you have to see it first, even if it is just in your mind's eye. This is where visualization comes in; it enables us to have a glimpse of what our desired future is like. Visualization is a method of creating mental images of the future you want, and it is a proven method that helps to keep you motivated and prepared to go after your goals with passion and commitment. This ensures that your goals and dreams are made more real and increases your chances of reaching them.

Generally, there are two types of visualization which are usually used together to achieve the best results. The first method is called *process visualization* and it focuses on the activities you need to carry out before you can get your desired results. The focus is on finishing each task in a list of tasks required to achieve a bigger objective. So, let's say your goal is to run a marathon. Process visualization would entail splitting the entire track into sections and you will picture how you will run each section, down to the last section where you're tired, ready to quit and need to finish the race!

The second method of visualization is *outcome visualization* and it involves you focusing on the bigger objective. So, from the example, you would have a picture of you finishing the marathon in your mind and try to imagine how it would feel. You can hear the crowd screaming and a lot of cameras and people smiling cheering your name.

In both methods, you can picture how you would feel if each event was happening as you visualize them. They are both powerful methods on their own and when combined together, you will definitely get better results.

So, go ahead and create a vivid picture of you achieving your goals, picture all the steps you will take to achieve the goal and how you feel when you have achieved it. Create an image of the person you want to be and hold that image for a few minutes, supply details to the picture and always bring up the image in your mind.

You must embrace your right to start being this person. Make it a habit that you're going to change to be the person that you know you're meant to be. It takes time, but now that you are aware, your eyes are open and as you begin, you can see the things that need to change. You will begin to see your habits are changing.

There are four major principles that will determine the effectiveness of whatever visualization technique you choose to use:

1. **Words of Affirmation.** You need to set the goal in your mind, close your eyes and repeat your goals or intentions in your mind. You can

write words of affirmation in that regard; make it short and simple and straight to the point.

2. **Create Memories.** This requires that you create a vivid imagination of the future event you want in your mind. You need to make it as real as possible and involve all your major five senses. The more vivid the imagination is, the better the imprint that will be recorded in your mind. When you do this, your mind records the event as a memory and not just something you hope for. When you can relate with your goals as something that has already happened, then you can say the visualization process is almost done.

3. **Incorporate strong positive emotions.** Every memory you have elicits an emotion whenever you remember them, and this is what makes them so powerful. So, you have to make sure you evoke emotions in your visualization to make them real enough for your brain to store them up as a memory.
4. **Repeat. Repeat. Repeat.** The more you do something, the better you get at it. Try to include visualization in your daily routine until you start noticing changes in your confidence level, your behavior and attitude! The more you repeat the process, the more your brain interprets the memory as something that has

happened and soon enough, it will become your reality.

Visualization will help you reach your goals, it helps you to put things in perspective, provides clarity and improves your concentration and drive. When combined with hard work, consistency and the appropriate resources, you will be unstoppable. It is a potent tool that you can use to achieve your goals and it can help you create the future you desire.

My hope for you is that you will know yourself, that you will know yourself better today than you did yesterday and that you will take up the challenge I've given you today. I hope that you will embrace the fierce Venus Warrior that you have inside of you. Let her out. And never, EVER accept yourself as "enough" because that is bullshit. You're so much more.

CONCLUSION: THE VENUS WARRIOR

Congratulations on having come this far!

By now, you should have gotten a clear picture of what your Venus Warrior is, and how you can leverage on her to live your best life. But if it still appears somewhat unclear or foggy, don't panic. Just like I said in the preceding chapters, each person has a unique path and these principles and lessons are not time-bound. You can revisit each chapter and soak things in over and over again. Take all the time you need, warrior.

It is important that you find and embrace your inner Venus Warrior; this is the key to unlocking all your potentials and being set firmly on the path to achieving your life's goals and fulfilling your mission. Not only will you have a deeper meaning of life, but you'll be able to make a bigger impact in the world and fulfill that burning desire within you to live out your purpose. Of course, this is only effective if you are a believer and not a naysayer. You have to believe that these principles will work for you and be ready to commit to the process before you will get an unbelievable result.

There is no arguing that we all need to make some changes to our lives and how we approach our goals. While we could decide to wait for some specific time on our calendar before acting, the best time to get things done is now.

Today is the best day for you to start becoming aware of your Venus Warrior, to start exploring into every aspect of your life, identifying the things that need to be fixed and then taking the steps needed to fix them.

The foundation required to accomplish any of the things listed in this book is self-confidence and a commitment to the process, regardless of how much time it takes. I know that it can be overwhelming when there is a lot of work to do, making you to either give up at the very beginning, before you start or just when things seem like they are not working. Or you may be so excited to get started, that you go in without a plan and you end up failing.

In order to achieve the desired paradigm shift, you need to identify the things that are standing in your way, do a thoughtful reflection and draft out a plan of attack. The importance of a plan and proper guidance on this journey cannot be exaggerated.

The era of saying "I am enough" and using this as an excuse to remain complacent and fold your arms while life happens to you is over! You are in a new place now and the mantra is that "I am more than enough." It may take some getting used to, but believe me, a big change has started, and you are about to step into the best years of your life.

The past is just that, the past. It may have made you who you are today, but it should not hold so much power over you that it makes you doubt yourself today. The truth is that you are not a product of your past, rather you are a product of your actions. Everything is happening in the present: your thoughts and the reaction to those thoughts. So, it is within your power to determine the kind of hold that the memories of your past will have over you. You can either be a victim or you can take charge of your life and begin to call the shots.

You need to always remember that excuses will do more of holding you back from achieving your goal than anything else. So, you need to stop making excuses for why you are not making progress. Identify your most common excuses and take steps to eliminate them; start making moves without excuses. Of course this not be easy, in the beginning, but you need to do away with excuses in order to give your Venus Warrior full expression.

Visualization is a very important part of your journey; when you can see it in your mind's eye, it makes it easier for it to become a reality. But you should always remember that it is not a replacement for commitment and hard work and neither does visualization alone guarantee success. Rather, when you combine the right amount of passion with consistent effort, a strong support system made up of people who believe in you, and you are able to visualize the future you want, you will unlock one of the most powerful ways to achieve your life's goals.

You need to hold yourself accountable or have an accountability partner who will ensure that you are on track with your action plans. This will help ingrain a sense of seriousness and responsibility in you. Make sure the person is someone who is genuinely interested in you, and who will be there with you in the course of your journey.

You should also track your progress by writing down your achievements, no matter how little you think they are. This will help you keep track of everything you are doing, and it will also make sure the thoughts of your action plan are permanently etched in the deep recesses of your mind. Also, seeing your victories written out is a morale booster and will help increase your self-confidence.

In conclusion, it's okay to fail or fall while on this journey. The most important thing is for you to shake it off and get back on track. It does not matter how long it takes you to find and embrace your inner warrior, she's always there within you and is just waiting to come out. You are not under any kind of pressure, so fail as many times as you need to. But, promise me you will always get back up and come back better each time.

I am proud of you for coming this far, and I am confident that your Venus Warrior is ready to take on the world.

See you at the top!

Let's Go!

Your Sister Venus Warrior,

Liz.

www.ingramcontent.com/pod-product-compliance
Lightning Source LLC
Chambersburg PA
CBHW070643220526
45466CB00001B/272